1/13

Lexile: _____ 1040 L _____
AR/BL: _____ 6.9 _____
AR Points: _1.0_____

Comets, Asteroids, and Meteors

Stuart Atkinson

Heinemann
LIBRARY
Chicago, Illinois

www.capstonepub.com
Visit our website to find out
more information about
Heinemann-Raintree books.

To order:
☎ Phone 800-747-4992
⌨ Visit www.capstonepub.com
to browse our catalog and order online.

Edited by Nancy Dickmann and Laura Knowles
Designed by Steve Mead
Original illustrations © Capstone Global
    Library Ltd 2013
Picture research by Mica Brancic

Originated by Capstone Global Library Ltd
Printed and bound in China by CTPS

16 15 14 13 12
10 9 8 7 6 5 4 3 2 1

**Library of Congress Cataloging-in-
    Publication Data**
Atkinson, Stuart.
    Comets, asteroids, and meteors / Stuart
Atkinson.—1st ed.
        p. cm.—(Astronaut travel guides)
    Includes bibliographical references and index.
    ISBN 978-1-4109-4567-9 (hb)—ISBN 978-1-4109-
4576-1 (pb) 1. Comets—Juvenile literature. 2.
Asteroids—Juvenile literature. 3. Meteors—Juvenile
literature. I. Title.
    QB721.5.A85 2013
    523.6—dc23   2011038925

Acknowledgements
We would like to thank the following for permission
to reproduce photographs: American Museum of
Natural History p. 7 (D. Finnin); ESA pp. 5 top,
18; Geza Gyuk p. 32; © Iris Langheinrich (www.
nyrockman.com) p. 34; J. C. Casado p. 4; Leonid
Alekseyevich Kulik p. 35; Library of Congress
p. 13 (Prints and Photographs Division Washington,
D.C.); © Minoru Yoneto pp. 5 bottom, 12; NASA
pp. 9 (Howard Edin), 11 (JPL-Caltech/UCLA/McREL),
14 (International Space Station Imagery), 15, 20
(Credits: Montage by Emily Lakdawalla. Ida, Dactyl,
Braille, Annefrank, Gaspra, Borrelly: NASA/JPL/
Ted Stryk. Steins: ESA/OSIRIS team. Eros: NASA/
JHUAPL. Itokawa: ISAS/JAXA/Emily Lakdawalla.
Mathilde: NASA/JHUAPL/Ted Stryk. Lutetia: ESA/
OSIRIS team/Emily Lakdawalla. Halley: Russian
Academy of Sciences Ted Stryk. Tempel 1: NASA/
JPL / UMD. Wild 2: NASA/JPL.), 23 (JPL-Caltech/
UCLA/MPS/DLR/IDA), 24 (JPL-Caltech/UCLA/
MPS/DLR/IDA), 28 (JPL), 5 middle and 38 (Denise
Watt); Photoshot p. 17 (© UPPA); Science Photo
Library pp. 6 (Detlev Van Ravenswaay), 37 (Detlev
Van Ravenswaay), 39 (Mark Garlick), 8 (Tony &
Daphne Hallas); Shutterstock pp. 31 (© Stephen
Coburn), 36 (© Andrea Danti), 40-41 (© Martiin ||
Fluidworkshop).

Design image elements reproduced with permission
of Shutterstock/© argus/© MarcelClemens/
© MarcelClemens/© mmgemini.

Cover photograph of Earth in space with a flying
asteroid and abstract background reproduced with
permission of Shutterstock/© Molodec.

We would like to thank Geza Gyuk, Paolo Nespoli,
and ESA for their invaluable help in the preparation
of this book.

Every effort has been made to contact copyright
holders of material reproduced in this book. Any
omissions will be rectified in subsequent printings if
notice is given to the publisher.

Disclaimer
All the Internet addresses (URLs) given in this book
were valid at the time of going to press. However,
due to the dynamic nature of the Internet, some
addresses may have changed, or sites may have
changed or ceased to exist since publication. While
the author and publisher regret any inconvenience
this may cause readers, no responsibility for any
such changes can be accepted by either the author
or the publisher.

CONTENTS

Target: Earth! 4

What's Out There? 6

Planning Your Trip 14

Who's Going with You? 16

Interview with an Astronaut 18

Amazing Asteroid Adventure 20

Comet Encounter 26

Interview with an Astronomer ... 32

Why Should We Go? 34

Map of the Solar System 40

Timeline 42

Fact File 43

Glossary 44

Find Out More 46

Index 48

Some words are shown in bold, **like this**. You can find out what they mean by looking in the glossary.

DON'T FORGET

These boxes will remind you what you need to take with you on your big adventure.

NUMBER CRUNCHING

Don't miss these little chunks of data as you speed through the travel guide!

AMAZING FACTS

You need to know these fascinating facts to get the most out of your space safari!

WHO'S WHO?

Find out about the space explorers who have studied the universe in the past and today.

TARGET: EARTH!

Looking up at the sky on a beautiful, clear night, it all seems very peaceful out there in space. Nothing much seems to be happening. In reality, lots of dangerous stuff is flying around the **solar system**. Millions of chunks of rock, metal, and ice **orbit** the Sun. They are leftovers from the birth of the **planets** around 4.5 billion years ago. Sometimes we cross paths with them, which can be very dangerous. Earth is often escaping threats from all sides!

In 1997, Comet Hale-Bopp delighted sky-watchers all around the world with its beautiful twin tails.

WHAT CAN WE SEE?

Amazingly, we can actually see some of this "cosmic debris." On most nights, you can see a few **meteors**, or shooting stars, zipping across the sky. These are tiny bits of space dust burning up in the **atmosphere**. **Binoculars** will show you an **asteroid** or two. Asteroids are huge chunks of metal or stone orbiting the Sun like mini-planets. Every few years, a bright comet appears in the sky, with a beautiful, shining tail. Comets are enormous, dirty snowballs that travel around the Sun in long, looping orbits.

What would it be like to go out into space and look at some of these fascinating objects? Let's travel and find out!

Meet **astronaut** Paolo Nespoli on page 18.

Discover how we might use asteroids in the future on page 38.

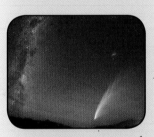

See page 12 to find out why comets are like "dirty snowballs."

DON'T FORGET

Meteors and comets are bright enough to be seen with just the human eye, but asteroids are so small and far away you really need a **telescope** to see them. Only the asteroid Vesta is both large enough and close enough to occasionally be visible as a tiny dot in the sky with just your eyes.

WHAT'S OUT THERE?

On a clear night, you will see at least a few shooting stars, as long as you are looking in the right direction at the right time. People used to think that shooting stars—called meteors by **astronomers**—really were stars falling to the ground. We now know that they are actually tiny grains of space dust, or **meteoroids**, burning up in the atmosphere.

During a meteor storm, hundreds or even thousands of shooting stars can be seen in just a few hours.

METEOR SHOWERS

During some special times of the year, you can see lots of shooting stars! During a meteor shower, dozens of shooting stars can flash across the sky every hour. They all come from the same direction, making them easier to see.

Pieces of space rock that are too big to burn up in the atmosphere fall to the ground as **meteorites**. It wasn't until the 1900s that people accepted that meteorites actually came from space. Before then, the Romans, Greeks, and other ancient people thought meteorites were gifts from sky gods. Even today, many people still make a wish when they see a shooting star. (There is no proof it works, but you can always try the next time you see one!)

In 1833, on the night of November 12–13, people across the United States were amazed and terrified as tens of thousands of shooting stars appeared in just a few hours, filling the night sky. This was one of the most intense meteor showers ever. People who saw this "Leonid Storm" said that shooting stars were "falling like snowflakes."

This meteorite, displayed in a New York museum, weighs about 15 tons!

SEEING SHOOTING STARS

Meteors appear as fast streaks of light in the sky. Most are quite faint, but sometimes really bright ones appear. These "fireballs" are small stones burning up in the atmosphere. When they are gone, they can leave glowing trails behind, which you can see through binoculars.

Watching meteors is very easy—you just need a clear night and somewhere dark to watch from. Because they can come from any direction at any time, the more sky you can see, the better. You might be lucky and see some from your backyard, but going to a park or out into the country will mean you will see lots more.

Many meteors can be seen in the night sky during the Leonid meteor shower.

If you are lucky and patient, you might see a bright meteor flashing across the sky.

WHEN TO WATCH

When Earth passes through a trail of space dust, we see a meteor shower, which can last for a few nights. The best ones are the Quadrantids (January), Perseids (August), Orionids (October), Leonids (November), and Geminids (December).

DON'T FORGET

You do not need any equipment to watch meteors—you just need your eyes. (Telescopes are useless because meteors move so fast.) Most meteors appear after midnight, so take an adult friend or relative with you. Dress appropriately, too—even the warmest summer night can turn chilly! Finally, you will need lots of patience. You can wait a long time to see a shooting star, then just as you are about to give up, you will see several in a row!

HUGE CHUNKS OF ROCK AND IRON

The first asteroid was discovered on January 1, 1801, by the Italian astronomer Giuseppe Piazzi, and then more were soon found. Early astronomers could only see asteroids as tiny dots in their telescopes, so they thought they were very distant, full-sized planets.

Eventually more powerful telescopes allowed astronomers to measure the asteroids' sizes and shapes. They found out that asteroids are actually much smaller than planets, so they were classed as "minor planets." Soon, astronomers taking lots of photographs of the night sky discovered there are thousands of asteroids orbiting the Sun.

AMAZING FACTS

Earth has had many close encounters with asteroids—some of them *too* close for comfort! In 2010, a pair of small space rocks actually passed between Earth and the Moon. In February 2011, asteroid 2011 CQ1 missed Earth by just 3,405 miles (5,480 kilometers)! But it was so small it would have burned up in the atmosphere anyway.

STUDYING ASTEROIDS

Modern astronomers use **radio telescopes** to watch asteroids that come close to Earth. **Space probes** regularly visit and study asteroids in deep space, taking amazing pictures of their strangely shaped bodies and **cratered** surfaces.

In 2011, the *Dawn* space probe took incredible images of the asteroid Vesta, showing a huge crater at its south pole and bizarre grooves and trenches curving around its body.

NUMBER CRUNCHING

Most asteroids orbit the Sun in a wide band between the planets Mars and Jupiter called the **asteroid belt**. However, there are many others scattered across the whole solar system. We now know of at least half a million asteroids in our solar system, but there must be many more we have not found yet.

When Comet Hyakutake passed unusually close to Earth in 1996, it became very bright to the human eye, and its tail crossed half the sky. Measurements by the *Ulysses* space probe revealed the tail was more than 342 million miles (550 million kilometers) long. That is almost four times the distance from Earth to the Sun!

DIRTY SNOWBALLS

For thousands of years, people were terrified whenever comets appeared in the sky. They thought they were signs that something awful was about to happen, and they blamed them for wars, disease, and earthquakes!

Thanks to telescopes and space missions, we now know that comets are just chunks of dirty ice traveling slowly around the Sun. If they get too close to the Sun, they start to melt. This releases gas and dust, which forms a shining tail.

Comet McNaught was very bright in the sky in 2007.

COMING BACK

The astronomer Edmond Halley was the first to figure out that comets can reappear in our sky more than once. The most famous comet of all now bears his name. Halley's Comet passes Earth every 76 years. Maybe you will see it in 2061!

When Halley's Comet appeared in 1910, many people were still afraid of comets.

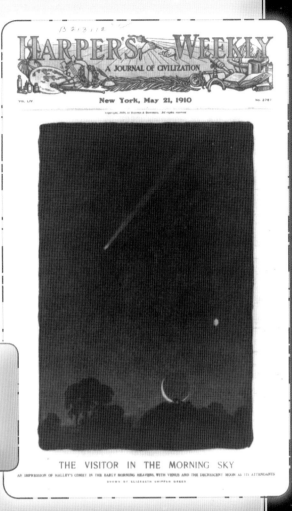

HARPER'S WEEKLY
A JOURNAL OF CIVILIZATION

New York, May 21, 1910

THE VISITOR IN THE MORNING SKY
AN IMPRESSION OF HALLEY'S COMET IN THE EARLY MORNING HEAVENS, WITH VENUS AND THE DECRESCENT MOON AS ITS ATTENDANTS
DRAWN BY ELIZABETH SHIPPEN GREEN

AMAZING FACTS

When Halley's Comet returned in 1910, astronomers calculated that Earth would pass through its tail. Having heard that the tail contained tiny amounts of poisonous gas, many people panicked. Some bought gas masks, fake "comet pills," and even umbrellas from con men who told them they would offer them protection! But there was never really any danger.

Seeing meteors is easy—just look up on a clear night and wait! You can see meteorites in museums. But if you want to see an asteroid or comet up close, you will need a spaceship to take you to one. Because it would need to carry food and fuel for a journey of up to a year, your ship would have to be quite big.

NUMBER CRUNCHING

If you flew to an asteroid in the asteroid belt, it could take you almost a year, as they are 186 to 373 million miles (300 to 600 million kilometers) away. That is between two and four times farther from the Sun than Earth is. It would be a lot quicker to travel to one of the asteroids that come close to Earth, which might be reached in a few weeks.

The inside of your spaceship would be full of equipment, just like inside the **International Space Station**.

You will also need special scientific supplies such as a spacesuit, cameras, and drilling equipment. Don't forget to take your favorite music, movies, and books to keep you entertained, or you will be bored to tears looking out of the window at nothing for months! Asteroids in the asteroid belt are so far apart that it is very unlikely you will fly into one accidentally.

DON'T FORGET

With deadly temperatures, no air, and no water, space is a very dangerous place. Your spacesuit is like a personal spaceship, carrying air and water and keeping you warm or cool. Its layers act as shields against tiny meteorites and **radiation** while you are outside the spacecraft.

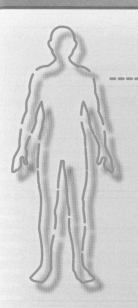

WHO'S GOING WITH YOU?

It is easy to get lonely on a long space journey. Why not take someone along who will keep you company and give you advice? Here are some suggestions.

CREW MEMBER:

GIUSEPPE PIAZZI (1746–1826)

Piazzi discovered the first asteroid, Ceres, in 1801. He would be able to tell you all about using telescopes to discover and observe asteroids in the time before space exploration began.

POTENTIAL JOB:

Mission historian/lookout

CREW MEMBER:

EDMOND HALLEY (1656–1742)

Halley was the first astronomer to predict the same comet could appear in the sky more than once. He calculated the orbits of comets seen in the sky many years apart. He could help plot your course.

POTENTIAL JOB:

Mission navigator

CREW MEMBER:

MINER

A miner works underground, so he or she could give you tips on staying safe in dangerous, rocky places. A miner would also have great advice about how to use and repair your drilling equipment.

POTENTIAL JOB:

Mission engineer and safety expert

CREW MEMBER:

ERNEST SHACKLETON (1874–1922)

Shackleton led an expedition to the ice-covered Antarctic in 1914. When their ship became trapped in ice and sank, Shackleton and his crew were forced to take shelter on a tiny island. Shackleton never gave up, and against incredible odds his crew survived. Shackleton's experience with snow and ice would be useful on a comet.

POTENTIAL JOB:

Extreme environment survival expert

CREW MEMBER:

MAJOR EILEEN COLLINS (BORN 1956)

Major Collins became the first female space shuttle pilot in 1995. She has traveled into space four times, with a total of more than 872 hours in space. If she were on your crew, she would be able to fly your spacecraft to a safe landing!

POTENTIAL JOB:

Mission pilot/commander

INTERVIEW WITH AN ASTRONAUT

Paolo Nespoli is an Italian **astronaut** with the **European Space Agency (ESA)**. He enjoys scuba diving, flying airplanes, and photography. In 2007, Paolo went into space for 15 days, and in 2010 he spent another 6 months in space. He has never visited an asteroid, but he has orbited Earth an amazing 2,782 times.

Q *Once you are selected as an astronaut, what is the training like?*

A The first couple of years after my selection, I did training; we do what is called "the basic training," where you essentially learn most of what it takes to be an astronaut: to fly in space, to handle the spacecraft and all the system's robotic arms, space walks, these kind of things. And then you enter into a kind of "parking area," waiting for your flight assignments. And then eventually you get assigned to a flight and then you start with a period, which could be two, three, four, or five years, in which you actually get qualified for that specific flight.

Q What was the hardest part of your astronaut training?

A Well, I like to travel, I like to move around, I like to do things, but when you do it two years, three years in a row, continuously, and you live out of a suitcase for a couple of months, it gets a little bit tiring. It's also hard, the fact that you are constantly under scrutiny. You jump to Russia and have your lessons, and then take an exam, and then you have another exam, and then you move to Japan and you take a couple of lessons, then you have an exam again. But you know, these are all things that eventually don't kill you, and I think make you better and prepare you really well for being in space.

Q Once you are up in space, how do you keep in touch with people on Earth?

A It's relatively easy to talk to or get in touch with people. We do have e-mail, we do have a sort of telephone, where we can call people. We do have a video conferencing system, which is used once a week to allow us to get in touch with the family, so you can see each other on video. What is missing a little bit is the time. For example, I was working between seven o'clock in the morning until, you know, ten or eleven o'clock in the evening, and then eventually, you get to do a little bit of e-mail, a few pictures; I was doing Twitter a little bit, until maybe one o'clock at night.

AMAZING ASTEROID ADVENTURE

It is hard to study asteroids from Earth, because they are so small and far away. It wasn't until space probes such as *Dawn* and *Hayabusa* started visiting asteroids that we learned more about them. These missions proved that asteroids are huge chunks of ancient space debris, battered after billions of years of being smashed into by other space rocks.

Asteroids come in a huge variety of shapes and sizes.

THE SCIENCE OF ASTEROIDS

Asteroids orbit the Sun like miniature planets. They are basically the leftover building blocks of planets that never formed, back at the birth of the solar system. They range in size from several feet to many miles across. Most are grouped together in a belt between Mars and Jupiter, but there are other smaller collections of them scattered throughout the solar system.

There are three main types of asteroids, each given a letter. "C" asteroids are dark and made of rock, "S" asteroids are made of stone and iron, and "M" asteroids are made just of metal. The first asteroid found, Ceres, was named after the Roman goddess of farming. Today, names like "James Bond" and "Arthur" are more common, because the person who discovers an asteroid can choose its name.

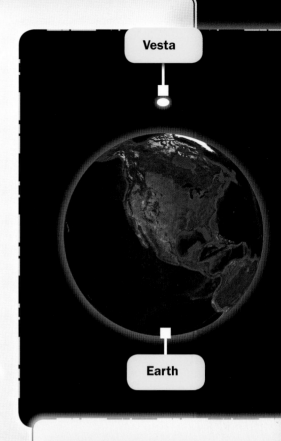

Vesta

Earth

Vesta is around 329 miles (530 kilometers) wide, compared to Earth's **diameter** of 7,926 miles (12,756 kilometers).

WHO'S WHO?

NASA scientist Eugene Shoemaker studied asteroid **impacts**. He trained astronauts for the Apollo Moon expeditions and is the only person to have been buried on the Moon: some of his ashes were carried there onboard the *Lunar Prospector* space probe. The asteroid probe *NEAR-Shoemaker* was named after him.

TOUCHDOWN!

As your spaceship approaches an asteroid, you would see it grow from a pinpoint of light in the distance to a bright star-like point of light. When you get close enough, you would see it as a huge, gray-black, potato-shaped rock, covered with craters and boulders. Some asteroids are more or less spherical (ball-shaped), but smaller ones often have irregular shapes.

After landing, you would put on your spacesuit, open the hatch, and step outside. But you would not climb down a ladder to the surface. **Gravity** is the force that pulls objects together. Earth's gravity is what keeps us on the ground. But because gravity on an asteroid is much weaker, you would float down to the ground in slow motion, like a feather!

DON'T FORGET

Because the gravity on even the largest asteroids would be a lot weaker than on Earth, you would be able to leap across the surface and jump upward a long way. But it might be a good idea to tie yourself to the surface, in case you got carried away—literally! Even if you were in no real danger, it might feel like you are jumping off into space.

THE ASTEROID'S SURFACE

Once you land on the surface, you will see that the ground beneath your boots is covered with a thick layer of dark, powdery dust. Boulders, rocks, and stones would be scattered all around you. You might see low hills in the distance, but because asteroids are so small, your **horizon** would seem very close. It would curve away from you steeply, too, which might make you feel a little space-sick!

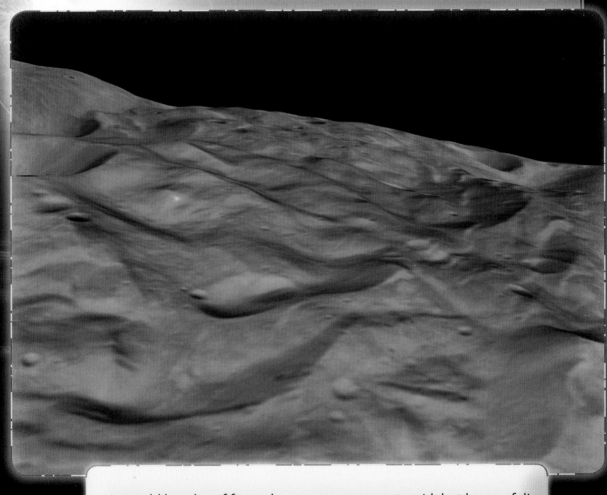

It would be a lot of fun to bounce across an asteroid, but be careful!

An Asteroid Safari

Once you have landed on the asteroid, you will be eager to explore your new surroundings. However, you will have to be careful and move slowly while you get used to the asteroid's low gravity.

If you land on Eros, you will be able to go over and look at the old *NEAR* space probe that landed on it in 2001. But look out for hidden dangers while you are sightseeing. If you trip on the space rocks littering the landscape, you might break equipment or damage your space helmet. Luckily, the weak gravity would probably stop you from falling into craters or cracks in the ground.

The *NEAR* space probe has shown us really detailed images of the asteroid Eros.

LOOKING BACK HOME

If you look up at the sky at the right time, you will see a breathtaking view of the Sun blazing brilliantly in a jet-black sky. At night you will see thousands of stars. And you might be really lucky and see Earth as a bright blue dot in the sky. You would not see many more asteroids, however. Even in the thickest part of the belt, asteroids are usually very, very far apart.

In February 2001, the *NEAR* (Near Earth Asteroid Rendezvous) probe landed on the 20.5-mile- (33-kilometer-) long asteroid Eros. During its amazingly successful mission, *NEAR* took 160,000 pictures of Eros's surface, showing more than one million boulders the size of a house or larger. The landing was a bonus because *NEAR* had only been designed to fly around the asteroid and not touch down on its surface.

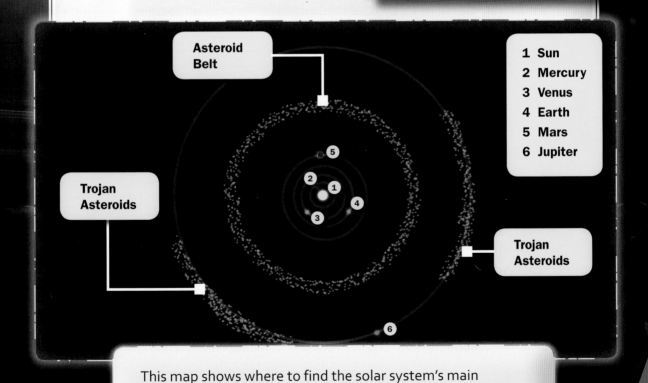

Asteroid Belt

Trojan Asteroids

Trojan Asteroids

1 Sun
2 Mercury
3 Venus
4 Earth
5 Mars
6 Jupiter

This map shows where to find the solar system's main groups of asteroids.

COMET ENCOUNTER

Most comets are never seen. They are usually so far from the Sun that they are always in darkness and freezing cold. Occasionally, a comet comes close enough to the Sun for its ice to melt, releasing dust and gas that form a glowing tail. Then we see it shining briefly in our sky, before it heads back out into space.

THE SCIENCE OF COMETS

The solid, icy center of a comet is the **nucleus**. They can measure from several hundred feet to many miles across. Surrounding that is a cloud of gas and dust called the coma. More gas and dust streams away from the nucleus to form the tail. Like asteroids, comets are leftovers from the birth of the solar system.

WHO'S WHO?

Comet Hale-Bopp was named after the two people who discovered it. Alan Hale was an experienced comet-hunter who spent hundreds of hours searching for comets with his telescope. Thomas Bopp was using a friend's telescope when he found the comet. Since both men found the comet at the same time, it shares their name. You can see photo of the comet on page 4.

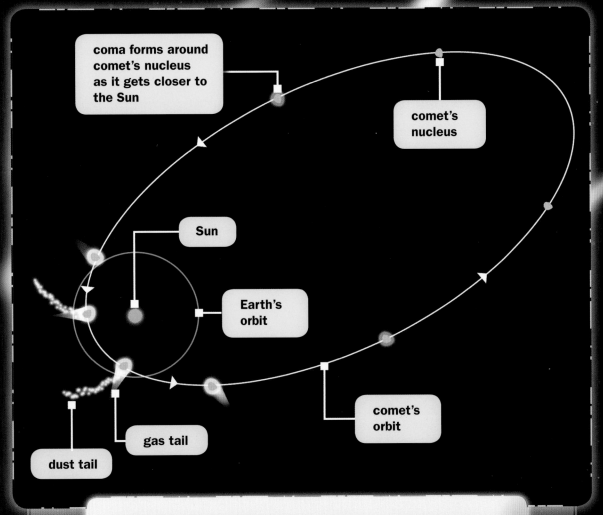

coma forms around
comet's nucleus
as it gets closer to
the Sun

comet's
nucleus

Sun

Earth's
orbit

comet's
orbit

gas tail

dust tail

This shows how a comet orbits the Sun. A comet's tail is always pushed away from the Sun, so sometimes comets can appear to be flying tail-first.

STUDYING COMETS

Comets can get very bright in the sky, and telescopes can see some detail in their tails. It wasn't until space probes started visiting comets in the late 1980s that we saw them up close. We now know that some comets are more like big piles of icy rubble held together by gravity than single, solid objects.

APPROACH AND LANDING

As you fly toward your comet, you will first see it as a large, fuzzy patch of light, with a misty tail streaming away from it. Soon you will see its nucleus emerging from the haze: a black-gray, lumpy body with clouds of gas and dust gushing out of it.

A comet's nucleus can be between several hundred feet and 12 miles (20 kilometers) across. If it were a small comet, with weak surface gravity, you might need to fire spikes from your ship to anchor you in place as you come in to land.

This image shows layers of dust surrounding a comet's solid center. The layers are not really these colors, but scientists show them this way to make them clearer.

an ICY LANDSCAPE

Just like on the asteroid, you could float down the ladder to land on the ice and frost. The dark landscape is an incredible sight. Craters both big and small cover the surface. You might also see spires and twisted columns of ice reaching up into the sky. They might be coated with dark dust or be stained dark by energy from the Sun. You might also see jets of icy vapor and dust shooting out of cracks in the frozen ground.

AMAZING FACTS

Comets are a possible source of water on Earth. Many astronomers believe that comets or icy asteroids crashed into Earth soon after it was formed. The water they brought filled our oceans.

NUMBER CRUNCHING

Comets do not last forever. Every time Halley's Comet travels around the Sun, it loses 250 million tons of ice and dust! It has just 2,200 trips around the Sun left before it vanishes completely in 170,000 years. So don't forget to look for it in 2061!

VIEW FROM A COMET

If you landed on an active part of a comet, or when it was close to the Sun, the sky above you could be dimmed by the cloud of gas and dust surrounding it. But to make up for losing the stars, you might see a shining ring around the Sun and colorful mini-rainbow "sun dogs" on either side of it. These are caused by ice crystals bending sunlight in the sky.

A CHANGING SURFACE

A comet's surface is always changing. Chunks of ice might be rising into space after being dislodged from the comet's surface. When the *Deep Impact* probe flew past Comet Hartley 2 in 2010, it had a huge surprise. It found itself surrounded by a storm of icy particles and snowballs. Some of them were as big as soccer balls!

WHO'S WHO?

Malcolm Hartley is a British astronomer who works at an observatory in Australia. He discovered Comet Hartley 2 in 1986, and he has since discovered several more. When the *Deep Impact* probe flew by Comet Hartley 2, he was invited to NASA's mission control to watch what happened.

A comet's surface might be covered with hidden craters and cracks in the ground. The weak surface gravity will probably keep you from falling in, but it is best to keep a careful lookout. You will also need to watch out for jets of gas rising from the surface.

Unlike the bright white of the Arctic and Antarctic on Earth, a comet's landscape is filled with dark, gloomy ice.

AMAZING FACTS

In 2014, the European Space Agency's *Rosetta* probe will reach Comet 67P/Churyumov–Gerasimenko, after 10 years in space. A small **lander** will drop down onto the icy nucleus to study it and photograph it. *Rosetta* will then spend two years orbiting the comet as it heads toward the Sun.

INTERVIEW WITH AN ASTRONOMER

Geza Gyuk is the director of astronomy at the Adler **Planetarium** in Chicago, Illinois. Part of his work involves studying asteroids. He also works on educational exhibits and programs at the planetarium.

Q *What do you like best about your job, and why?*

A The best part of my job is getting to do something I love every day… and get paid for it. I love to learn about new things. I particularly like observing, especially when I get a chance to actually go to the observatory. I spend about half my time doing research and half my time working on educational projects.

Q *Why are you interested in asteroids?*

A Asteroids are the smallest rocky worlds, with a history that in some ways is similar to the Earth's and in some ways very different. We can learn a lot about how the solar system formed from studying them. And, of course, I've also just been intrigued ever since I first started reading science fiction with tales of visiting and mining asteroids.

Q *Do you think that, in the future, humans could use asteroids in some way?*

A I'm sure that we will! Eventually humanity will have a permanent presence in space and we'll need some source of raw materials. It doesn't make sense to haul everything up against thousands of miles of gravity when instead one can use material that is already in space!

Q *If you could travel anywhere in the universe, where would you like to go, and what would you hope to find?*

A I think that I'd like to travel to another Earth-like world. I'm sure that such worlds must exist and some of them will be in picturesque places. Perhaps the world might have multiple large moons, as has been suggested. I love to imagine sitting on the shores of an immense ocean with two moons looming overhead as the Sun sinks, revealing a majestic starscape hiding behind the blue skies.

Q *What advice would you give to readers who want to be astronomers?*

A The most important thing is to hold onto your sense of wonder. The universe is an amazing place, and your motivation for becoming an astronomer should be one of continuous excitement and joy at learning more about such a fantastic place. Certainly one doesn't become an astronomer for the money! Studying math and science is important, but don't neglect English and history. An astronomer also has to tell and excite other people about his or her discoveries!

WHY SHOULD WE GO?

It is important to learn as much as we can about asteroids and comets, because one day we may find that Earth is in danger from one of them. Science fiction movies and books love to destroy Earth with asteroids and comets. Could it really happen?

If Earth were ever hit, the damage would depend on the size of the object. A small meteorite cannot cause much more damage than make a hole through a roof. But an asteroid or comet bigger than 0.6 mile (1 kilometer) wide could easily destroy a city.

In 1992, a meteorite crashed into a car in New York.

Many experts believe that the dinosaurs were wiped out 65 million years ago when an asteroid about 6.2 miles (10 kilometers) wide hit Earth. If something that size landed in the ocean today, it could cause enormous waves called tsunamis and huge changes in our planet's weather. Humankind might become **extinct**, just like the dinosaurs did.

WATCHING THE SKY

Today, scientists search the sky for objects that might threaten Earth. When something is found, its path is calculated very carefully. So far these "Sky Surveys" have found over 1,200 objects that might possibly hit Earth one day, but no one has found any that definitely will.

A forest in Siberia was flattened in 1908 by the shock wave from an exploding comet or asteroid fragment.

SEARCH THE SKY, SAVE THE EARTH?

A huge crater in the United States is proof that Earth has been hit by asteroids before. The Meteor Crater is over 0.6 mile (1 kilometer) across. It was formed about 50,000 years ago, when an iron asteroid slammed into the Arizona desert. The asteroid was about 164 feet (50 meters) wide and weighed 300,000 tons. All wildlife in the area would have been wiped out by the impact and its after-effects.

This is what it might look like if a huge asteroid were headed straight toward Earth.

AMAZING FACTS

On August 10, 1972, crowds in the Grand Teton National Park, in Wyoming, were amazed to see a fireball racing across the sky. A small asteroid was skipping off Earth's atmosphere like a stone skimmed across a pond. Luckily, it bounced back off out into space, proving that our atmosphere protects us against smaller asteroids.

AVOIDING COMETS AND ASTEROIDS

If we found something similar on a collision course with Earth today, we might be able to make it change course. If we could fit a rocket engine to it, we could steer it away from our planet. Another idea is to paint one side black, to make heat from the Sun change its orbit!

We could also try blowing it up with bombs, but that might make things worse. Instead of one large rock hitting us, lots of smaller rocks would hit many different places across the planet, causing much more damage. We can prepare by learning as much as possible about asteroids and comets.

Instead of blowing up an Earth-threatening asteroid, we might just pull it off-course using special spaceships.

USING ASTEROIDS AND COMETS

Asteroids and comets may be useful to us in the future. One day, people might be able to capture asteroids out in deep space, then bring them back to Earth to be mined for precious metals and **minerals**. Other asteroids could be used as space stations if they are put into orbit around Earth or other planets. Asteroids orbiting the Sun could be used as "natural spaceships," to give explorers free rides around the solar system. It is even possible comets could be used as sources of water, to allow humans to live in space in the future.

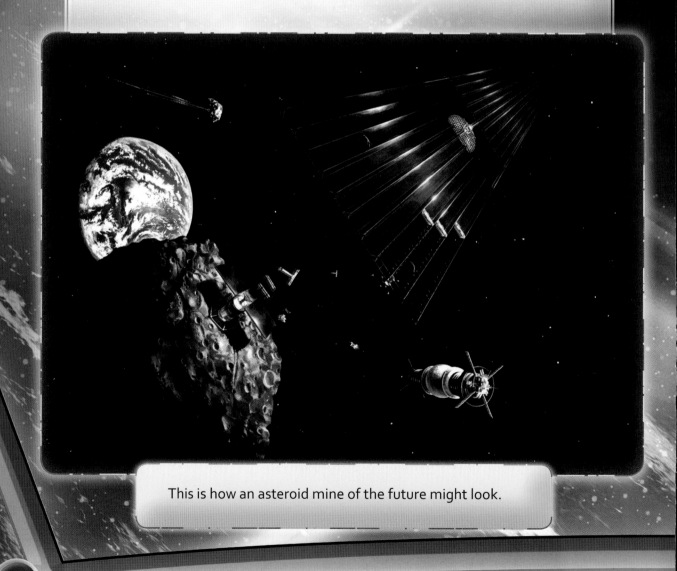

This is how an asteroid mine of the future might look.

MORE LIKE EARTH?

Some scientists even want to deliberately smash comets into Mars! They think it could be possible to make other planets more like Earth so people could live on them. Crashing comets into Mars could thicken its cold, thin atmosphere. This could make the planet warm enough for liquid water to exist on its surface. But such **terraforming** would take thousands of years, so don't hold your breath. But maybe people in the far future will hitchhike a ride on an asteroid to Mars and splash in comet rain when they get there!

Perhaps if we smashed icy comets into Mars, in the far future, the "Red Planet" might become a green and blue world.

MAP OF THE SOLAR SYSTEM

MERCURY

VENUS

EARTH

MARS

ASTEROID BELT

JUPITER

SATURN

URANUS

NEPTUNE

The sizes of the planets and their distances from the Sun are not to scale. To show all the planets' real distances from the Sun, this page would have to be over half a mile long!

TIMELINE

65 million years ago A large asteroid smashes into Earth, possibly contributing to the extinction of the dinosaurs.

1070–1080 Halley's Comet is pictured in the Bayeux Tapestry, which tells of events in English history from around 1066.

1705 Edmond Halley determines that comets seen in 1531, 1607, and 1682 were the same one and predicts its return in 1758. The comet arrives on schedule and is later named Halley's Comet.

1801 Giuseppe Piazzi discovers the first and largest asteroid, Ceres, orbiting between Mars and Jupiter.

1833 The Leonid meteor storm stuns observers in the United States.

1920 The Hoba meteorite is found in Africa. It is the largest found to date—at 60 tons!

1972 Crowds in Grand Teton National Park in Wyoming see a small asteroid skipping off Earth's atmosphere.

1991–1994 The *Galileo* spacecraft takes the first closeup images of an asteroid (Gaspra) and discovers the first moon (later named Dactyl) orbiting an asteroid (Ida).

1994 Fragments of comet Shoemaker-Levy 9 smash into Jupiter's atmosphere, leaving "bruises" bigger than Earth.

1996 Comet Hale-Bopp thrills observers worldwide with its beautiful double tail.

2001 The *NEAR-Shoemaker* space probe lands on the asteroid Eros at the end of its mission.

2006 Japan's *Hayabusa* becomes the first spacecraft to land on and take off from an asteroid. It also returns the first asteroid samples to Earth four years later.

2010 The *EPOXI* probe encounters Comet Hartley 2 and photographs "snowballs" shooting out of it.

2011 The *Dawn* spacecraft arrives at the asteroid Vesta and begins to study it, returning detailed images to Earth.

FACT FILE

OBJECT	DISTANCE FROM SUN	SIZE	FIRST SPACE AGE ENCOUNTER
Meteor	Meteors occur in Earth's atmosphere, so they are very close—in cosmic terms! But we now know meteors occur elsewhere in the solar system. The Mars *Exploration* rovers have photographed several shooting stars in the night sky of Mars.	The meteoroids that burn up in the atmosphere, producing meteors, range in size from a grain of dust to a small stone. Larger meteoroids, 3 feet (1 meter) or so in size, become "fireballs" that can be as bright as a full Moon!	Astronauts orbiting Earth actually look *down* on shooting stars! They see meteors burning up in the atmosphere hundreds of miles below them.
Asteroid	Most asteroids exist in a band, or "belt," that lies between Mars and Jupiter. If you set off to travel to this asteroid belt in a race car at 155 miles (250 kilometers) per hour, it would take you more than 100 years to get there!	The largest asteroid is Ceres. It is approximately 621 miles (1,000 kilometers) across. There are 16 known asteroids with diameters of 150 miles (240 kilometers) or more.	The first asteroid visited by a space probe was Gaspra in 1991. The *Galileo* space probe took many photos of it. *Galileo* went on to discover the first moon of an asteroid—Dactyl, which orbits the asteroid Ida. In 2011, NASA's *Dawn* probe began studying the asteroid Vesta. It will continue on to Ceres.
Comet	Most comets exist in the outer edges of our solar system in part of the original cloud of dust and gas left over from the birth of the solar system. For a comet to become bright to the human eye, it has to come close to Earth and the Sun at the same time, and not many do.	The solid center of a comet—its nucleus—is quite small, just a few miles across, but comet tails can grow to enormous sizes, sometimes millions of miles in length!	The first space probe to encounter a comet was the Russian *Vega 1*, in March 1986. It flew past Halley's Comet, taking images that revealed the nucleus was dumbbell- or peanut-shaped.

GLOSSARY

asteroid small object in the solar system that is traveling on its own path around the Sun

asteroid belt area between Mars and Jupiter where most asteroids can be found

astronaut man or woman who travels into space

astronomer person who studies space

atmosphere layer of gases surrounding a planet

binoculars two small telescopes joined together to make one low magnification instrument, which a person can look through

crater dish-shaped hole in the surface of a planet, made by a meteorite smashing into the surface

diameter width of a circle at its widest point

European Space Agency (ESA) European organization involved in space research and exploration

extinct no longer living

gravity force that pulls objects toward each other. Big objects, such as planets, have much stronger gravity than smaller objects, such as people.

horizon farthest part of the landscape you can see against the sky

impact when one object crashes into another

International Space Station large spacecraft orbiting Earth where astronauts from different countries live and work

lander small spacecraft that lands on the surface of a body in the solar system

meteor astronomical term for "shooting star"

meteorite piece of space rock or metal that has fallen to Earth

meteoroid small piece of rock, metal, or ice orbiting the Sun

mineral natural, solid substance found in the ground, such as gold

NASA short for "National Aeronautics and Space Administration," it is the U.S. space agency

nucleus central, solid part of a comet

orbit path of an object around a star or planet

planet large, roughly round body that orbits a star like the Sun

planetarium domed building in which images of stars and planets are projected for public entertainment or education

radiation particles and rays that come from some objects in space, such as stars. Some types of radiation are harmful to humans.

radio telescope telescope that collects radio waves and signals from space instead of rays of light

solar system the Sun, the planets, and other objects that are in orbit around it

space probe unmanned spacecraft that is sent to study an object in space

telescope device that makes distant objects look bigger

terraforming making a dead planet more like Earth so that life can exist there

FIND OUT MORE

BOOKS

Bond, Peter. *DK Guide to Space* (DK Guides). New York: Dorling Kindersley, 2006.

Goldsmith, Mike. *Solar System* (Discover Science). New York: Macmillan, 2010.

Graham, Ian. *What Do We Know About the Solar System?* (Earth, Space, and Beyond). Chicago: Raintree, 2011.

Lippincott, Kristen. *Astronomy* (Eyewitness). New York: Dorling Kindersley, 2008.

DVD

The Universe (A&E, 2010)

INTERNET SITES

FactHound offers a safe, fun way to find internet sites related to this book. All of the sites on FactHound have been researched by our staff.

Here's all you do:

Visit *www.facthound.com*

Type in this code: 9781410945679

PLACES TO VISIT

Hayden Planetarium
Central Park West and 79th Street, New York, N.Y. 10024
www.haydenplanetarium.org

Jet Propulsion Laboratory
4800 Oak Grove Drive, Pasadena, California 9110
www.jpl.nasa.gov

Meteor Crater
near Flagstaff, Arizona
www.meteorcrater.com

Smithsonian National Air and Space Museum
Independence Ave. at 7th St. SW, Washington, D.C. 20560
www.nasm.si.edu

FURTHER RESEARCH

If you enjoyed this book and want to learn more about
asteroids and comets, there is a lot you can do:

- Visit the library to find books about astronomy and space.
Choose books that are as up-to-date as possible—
new discoveries are made all the time!

- You can also ask at your local librarians about how to
contact your nearest astronomical society. This is a group
of people who are interested in the night sky. They will hold
regular meetings, where they discuss what is happening
in the world of astronomy and see the very latest pictures
from space. They will be happy to answer any questions you
might have and might be able to show you a real asteroid or
comet through one of their telescopes, too.

- Visit any local science museums, natural history museums,
or planetariums. There will probably be displays, exhibits,
and information about space exploration there.

INDEX

asteroid belt 11, 14, 15, 21, 25, 41
asteroid impacts 21, 34, 35, 36
asteroids 5, 10–11, 14, 15, 16, 20–25, 32–33, 34, 37, 38, 42, 43
astronauts 18–19, 21
astronomers 6, 10, 13, 16, 30, 32–33, 39
atmospheres 5, 36, 39

Bopp, Thomas 26

Ceres 16, 21
Collins, Major Eileen 17
coma 26, 27
Comet 67P/Churyumov-Gerasimenko 31
Comet Hale-Bopp 4, 26
Comet Hartley 2 30
Comet Hyakutake 12
comet tails 4, 5, 12, 13, 26, 27
comets 4, 5, 12–13, 14, 26–31, 34, 38, 39, 42, 43
craters 10, 11, 22, 29, 31, 36

Dawn space probe 11, 20
Deep Impact space probe 30
dinosaurs 35

Earth 22, 25, 29
Eros 24, 25
European Space Agency (ESA) 18, 31
extinction 35

gases 12, 28, 31
Geminids 9
gravity 22, 24, 27, 28, 31
Gyuk, Geza 32–33

Hale, Alan 26
Halley, Edmond 13, 16, 42
Halley's Comet 13, 29, 42
Hartley, Malcolm 30
Hayabusa space probe 20

ice 12, 17, 26, 29, 30, 31
International Space Station 14

Leonids 7, 9

Mars 39, 40
metals and minerals 21, 38
Meteor Crater 36
meteor showers 6, 7, 9
meteorites 7, 14, 15, 34, 42
meteoroids 6
meteors 5, 6–9, 14, 43
Moon 21

NASA 21, 30
NEAR space probe 21, 24, 25
Nespoli, Paolo 18–19
nucleus 26, 27, 28

orbit 4, 5, 11, 16, 21, 27, 37
Orionids 9

Perseids 9
Piazzi, Giuseppe 10, 16, 42
planets 4, 21, 39

Quadrantids 9

radiation 15
radio telescopes 10
Rosetta space probe 31

Sagan, Carl 39
Schweickart, Rusty 35
Shackleton, Ernest 17
Shoemaker, Eugene 21
shooting stars *see* meteors
Sky Surveys 35
solar system 4, 11, 21, 26, 40–41
space debris 4, 5, 20
space probes 10, 11, 12, 20, 21, 24, 25, 30, 31, 42
space shuttles 17
space stations 14, 38
spacecraft 14, 17, 37
spacesuits 15
stars 25
Sun 4, 5, 11, 21, 25, 26

terraforming 39
tsunamis 35

Ulysses space probe 12

Vesta 5, 11, 21

watching asteroids 14
watching comets 14
watching meteors 8, 9
water 29, 38, 39